The Wednesday Group

Bealaí Ealaíonta

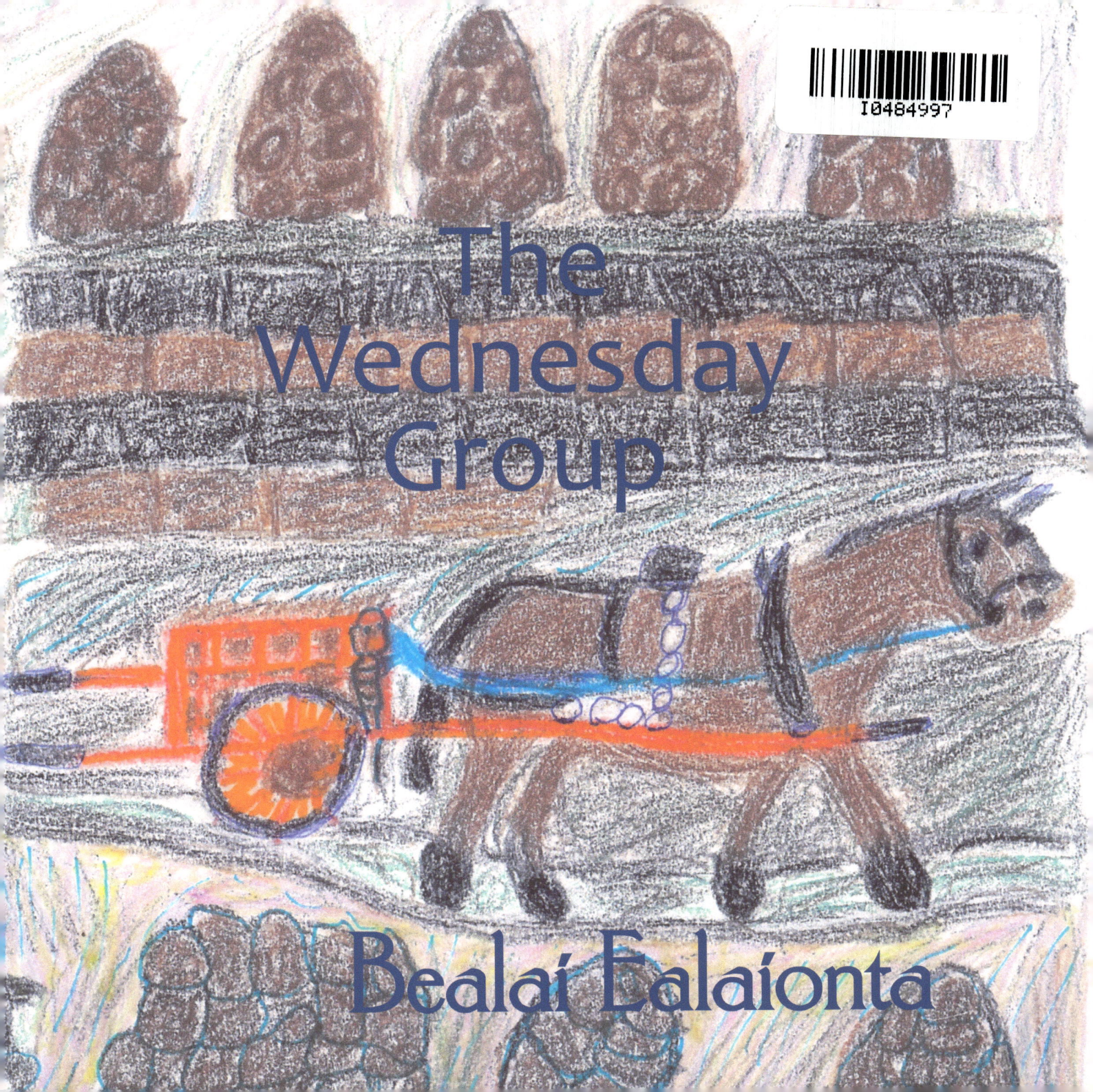

Bealaí Ealaíonta
(Artful Paths)

Cover: Dora O'Connor,
from a drawing by Ellen O'Donnell

Title page: Ellen O'Donnell

Text written by
Kristi Collins, Úna Ní Shé and
The Wednesday Group

Photographs by
Úna Ní Shé

Design by
Kristi Collins and Úna Ní Shé

Layout by
Kristi Collins

Artwork by
Kay Finn, Maryanne Landers,
Bríd Ní Shéaghdha, Nóra NicGearailt,
Dora O'Connor, Ellen O'Donnell,
Anna O'Kelly, Lily O'Regan,
Mícheál O Séaghdha and Caitlín Uí Chathaláin

Preface

Every second Wednesday for several years, people have been gathering at Gairdín Mhuire Day Care Centre in Dingle to participate in classes facilitated by artist Úna Ní Shé.

The members of this Wednesday ensemble share a lifetime of creativity and artistry, each making important contributions to the culture of their local community in Corca Dhuibhne and to wider Irish society. There has been little public recognition of the intrinsic artistic value of their craftsmanship, skills and knowledge, or their impact on our cultural and artistic heritage.

The Wednesday Group is part of the *Bealaí Ealaíonta series* — four volumes which showcase work by the unsung artists of Corca Dhuibhne.

This volume examines the artistic processes of the participants and includes stories from the artists themselves, providing glimpses of the many cultural influences they have drawn upon in the creation of their work.

Most of all, it celebrates the members of Wednesday Group ensemble as contemporary, active arts practitioners within their local community.

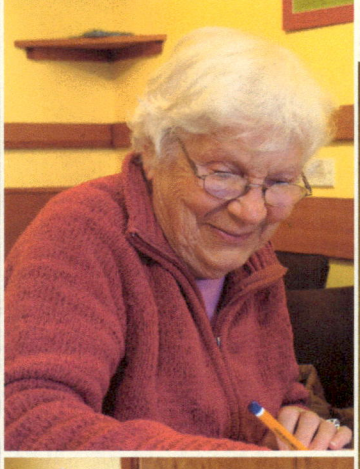

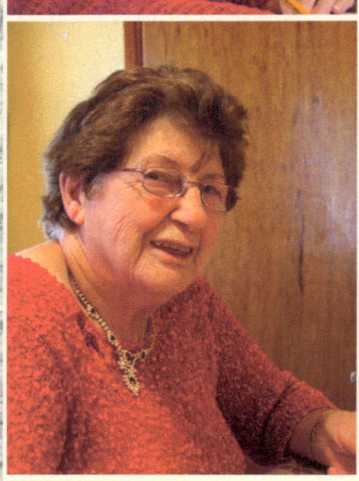

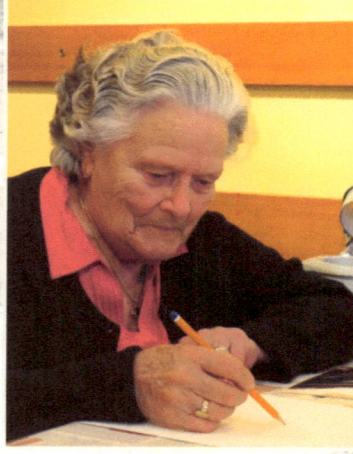

The Wednesday Group

Each artist of the Wednesday Group brings a unique set of life experiences and influences to their work.

Some were born in Corca Dhuibhne and have spent their whole lives immersing themselves in the local community, never really going away.

Others were adults when they chose to make Corca Dhuibhne their home, carrying with them the memories and influences of childhoods spent in other parts of Ireland.

Some have spent much of their adult lives away from Ireland, and in the Wednesday Group they are able to re-establish contact and build relationships with people who share their sense of time and place, and whose memories of growing up resonate with their own. Coming back into each other's lives as older people brings with it the comfort of being known, and remembered.

The artists in the group each engage in distinct and particular ways with their local environment, their family and community, and draw on different elements of these experiences in their art.

The common narrative thread that ties the work together is the fact that it is directly informed by their daily lives. The finished pieces are not exercises in nostalgia, although they may contain memories and elements of the past.

Without exception they are grounded firmly in the context of everyday life on the Peninsula, both then and now. There is an absence of work within the group that illustrates the time they have spent in other places.

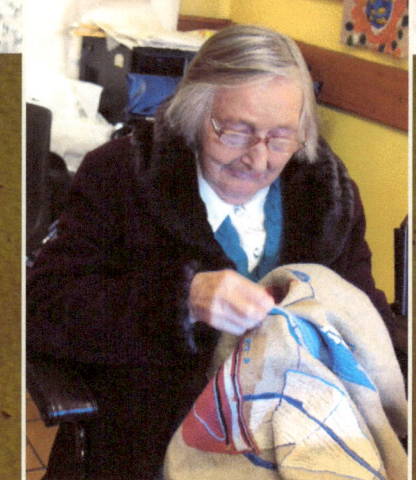

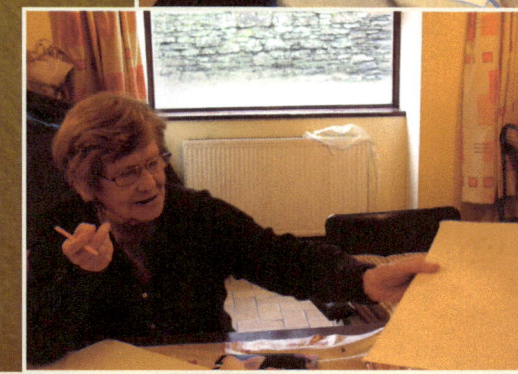

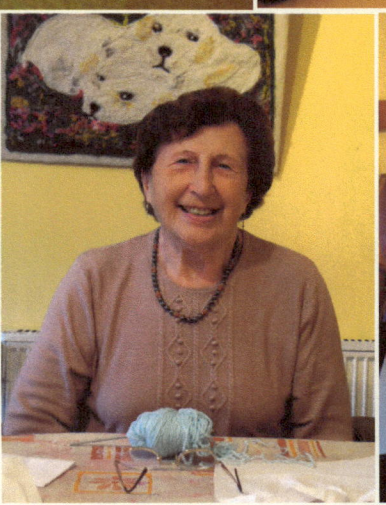

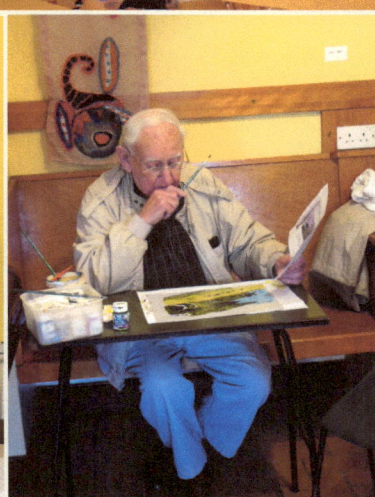

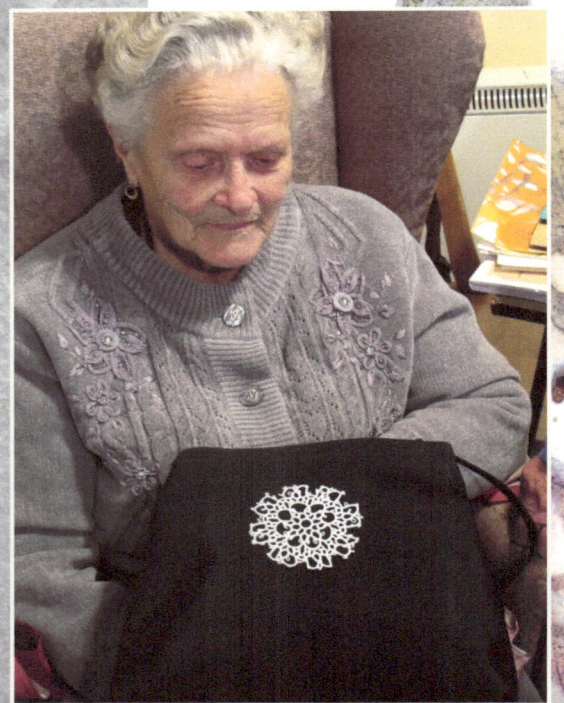

The variety of media the Wednesday Group engage with in their artistic practice, and the quality of the work produced, reflects the culture that first influenced and inspired them.

They are creative in everything they do, drawing on the traditional skills and techniques acquired in their childhoods to continually construct and transform, design and forge.

The skills once necessary for day-to-day living have been honed and developed in new ways and different contexts. Evident in their art pieces is a philosophy that embraces hard work and productivity, centred round the belief that "you get out what you put in."

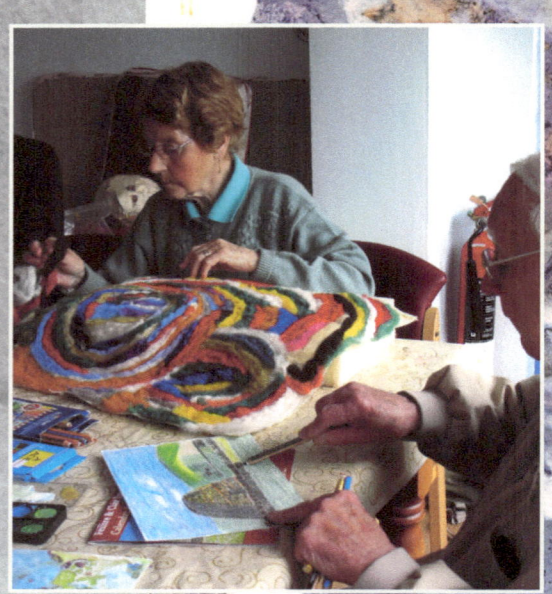

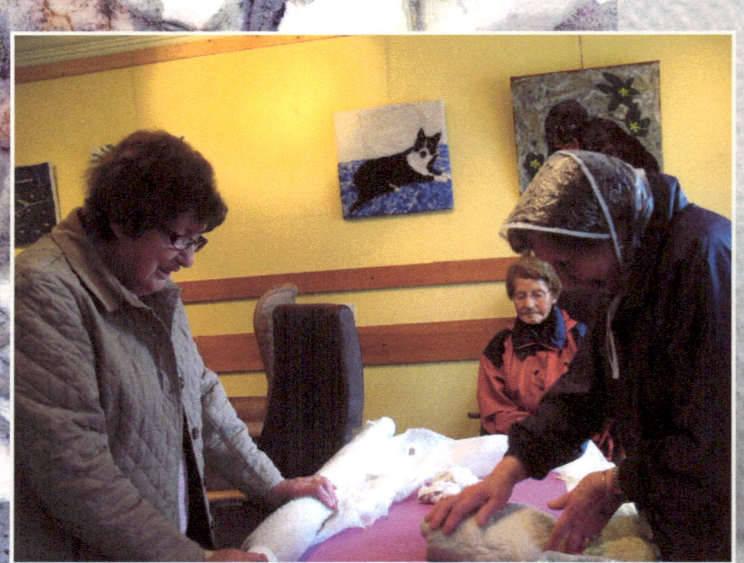

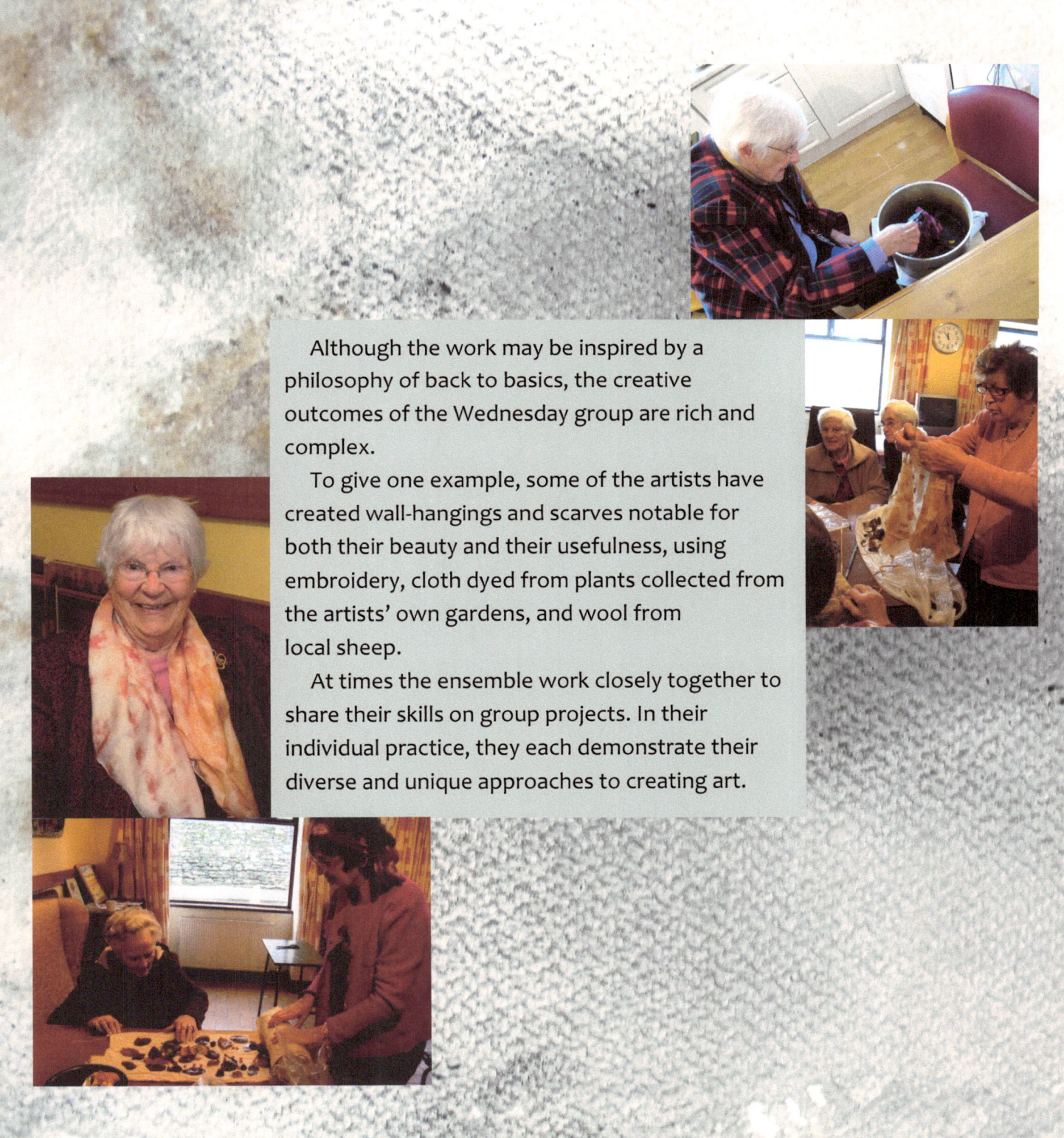

Although the work may be inspired by a philosophy of back to basics, the creative outcomes of the Wednesday group are rich and complex.

To give one example, some of the artists have created wall-hangings and scarves notable for both their beauty and their usefulness, using embroidery, cloth dyed from plants collected from the artists' own gardens, and wool from local sheep.

At times the ensemble work closely together to share their skills on group projects. In their individual practice, they each demonstrate their diverse and unique approaches to creating art.

Artist Profiles

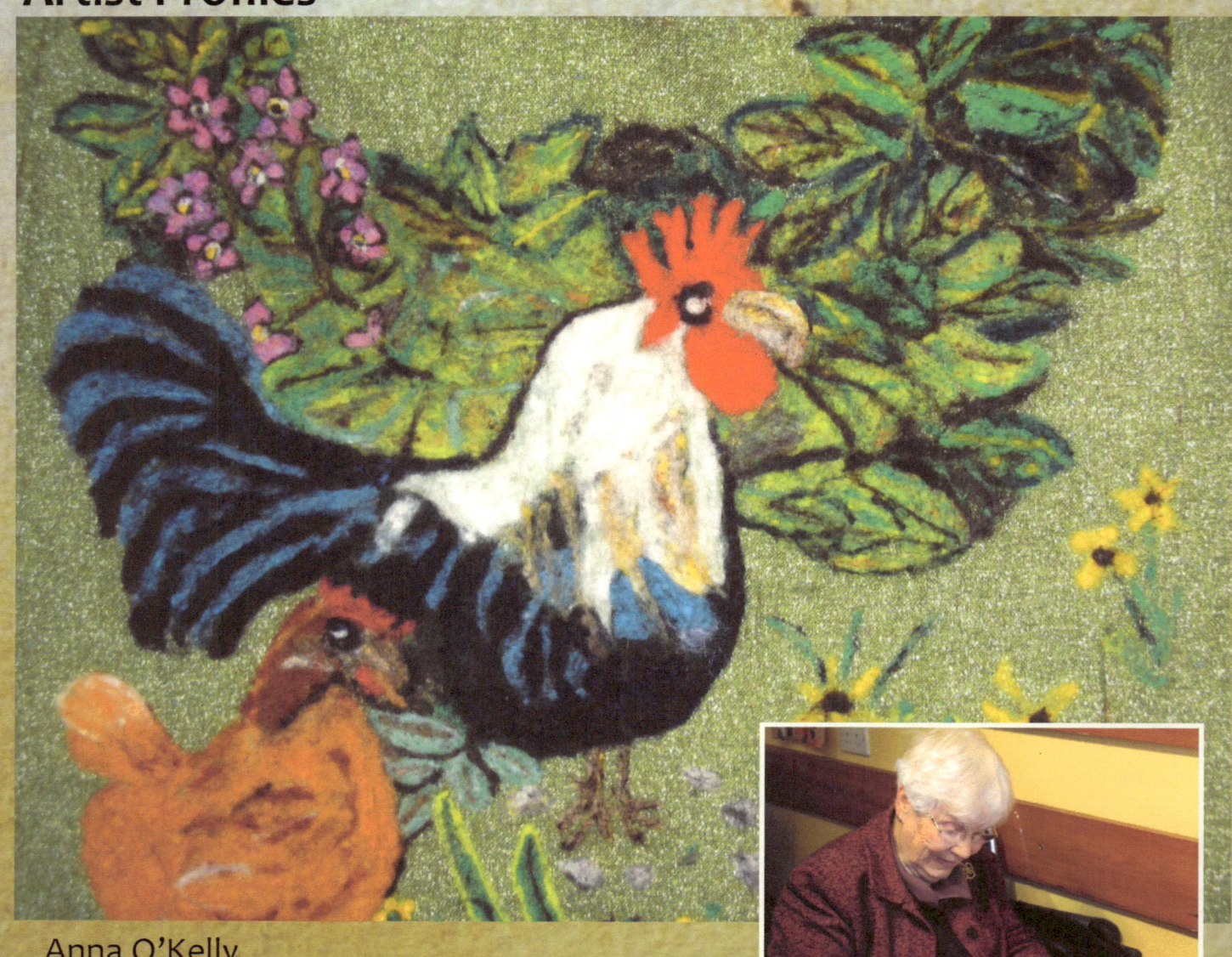

Anna O'Kelly

Anna's art is informed by her family and the experiences they have shared; a love of gardening she inherited from her father, a love of design fostered by her mother, and memories of holidays with her husband and children, many of them spent in the place she now calls home.

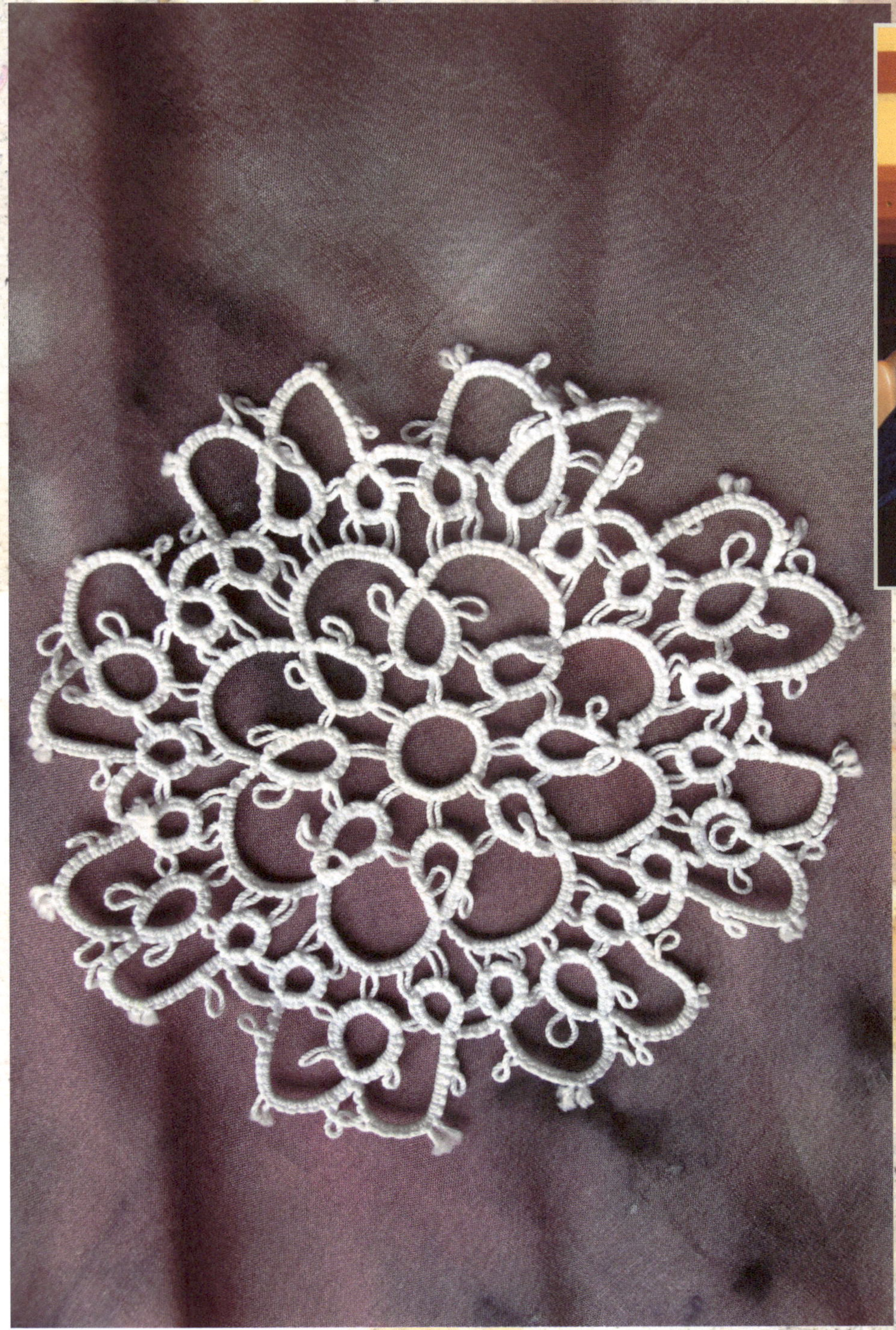

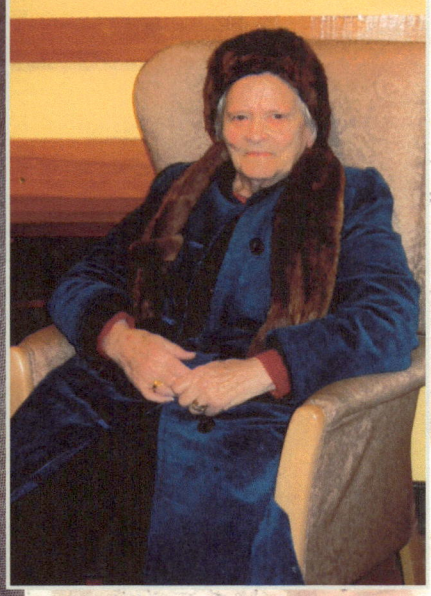

Bríd Ní Shéaghdha

Bríd is descended from generations of maker-women, respected and knowledgeable members of the local community who passed on their skills to their children and grandchildren.
Her identity is intertwined with Com Dhíneol, the townland where she was raised, and this strong sense of place is evident in her landscapes of the area.

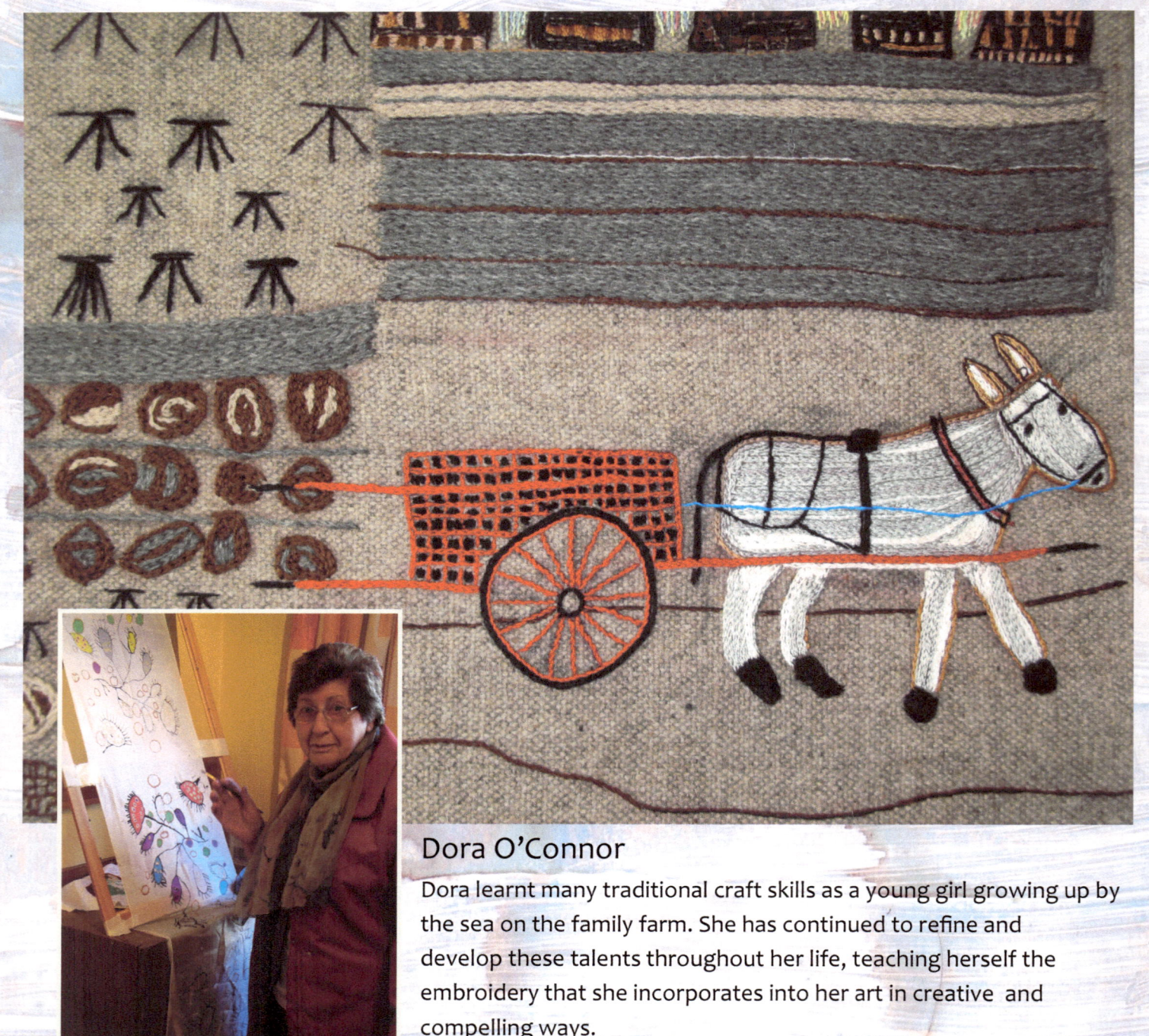

Dora O'Connor

Dora learnt many traditional craft skills as a young girl growing up by the sea on the family farm. She has continued to refine and develop these talents throughout her life, teaching herself the embroidery that she incorporates into her art in creative and compelling ways.

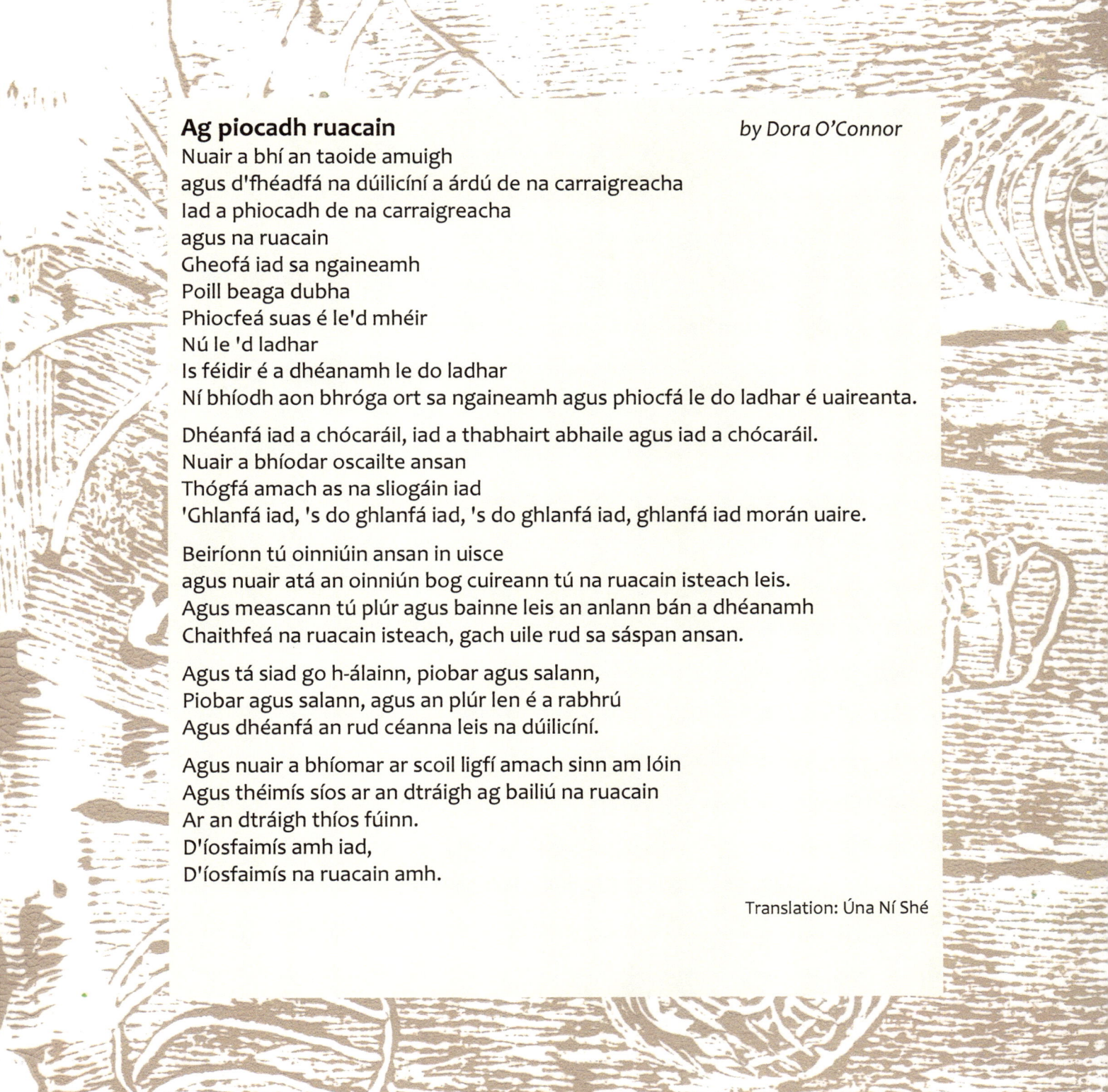

Ag piocadh ruacain
by Dora O'Connor

Nuair a bhí an taoide amuigh
agus d'fhéadfá na dúilicíní a árdú de na carraigreacha
Iad a phiocadh de na carraigreacha
agus na ruacain
Gheofá iad sa ngaineamh
Poill beaga dubha
Phiocfeá suas é le'd mhéir
Nú le 'd ladhar
Is féidir é a dhéanamh le do ladhar
Ní bhíodh aon bhróga ort sa ngaineamh agus phiocfá le do ladhar é uaireanta.

Dhéanfá iad a chócaráil, iad a thabhairt abhaile agus iad a chócaráil.
Nuair a bhíodar oscailte ansan
Thógfá amach as na sliogáin iad
'Ghlanfá iad, 's do ghlanfá iad, 's do ghlanfá iad, ghlanfá iad morán uaire.

Beiríonn tú oinniúin ansan in uisce
agus nuair atá an oinniún bog cuireann tú na ruacain isteach leis.
Agus meascann tú plúr agus bainne leis an anlann bán a dhéanamh
Chaithfeá na ruacain isteach, gach uile rud sa sáspan ansan.

Agus tá siad go h-álainn, piobar agus salann,
Piobar agus salann, agus an plúr len é a rabhrú
Agus dhéanfá an rud céanna leis na dúilicíní.

Agus nuair a bhíomar ar scoil ligfí amach sinn am lóin
Agus théimís síos ar an dtráigh ag bailiú na ruacain
Ar an dtráigh thíos fúinn.
D'íosfaimís amh iad,
D'íosfaimís na ruacain amh.

Translation: Úna Ní Shé

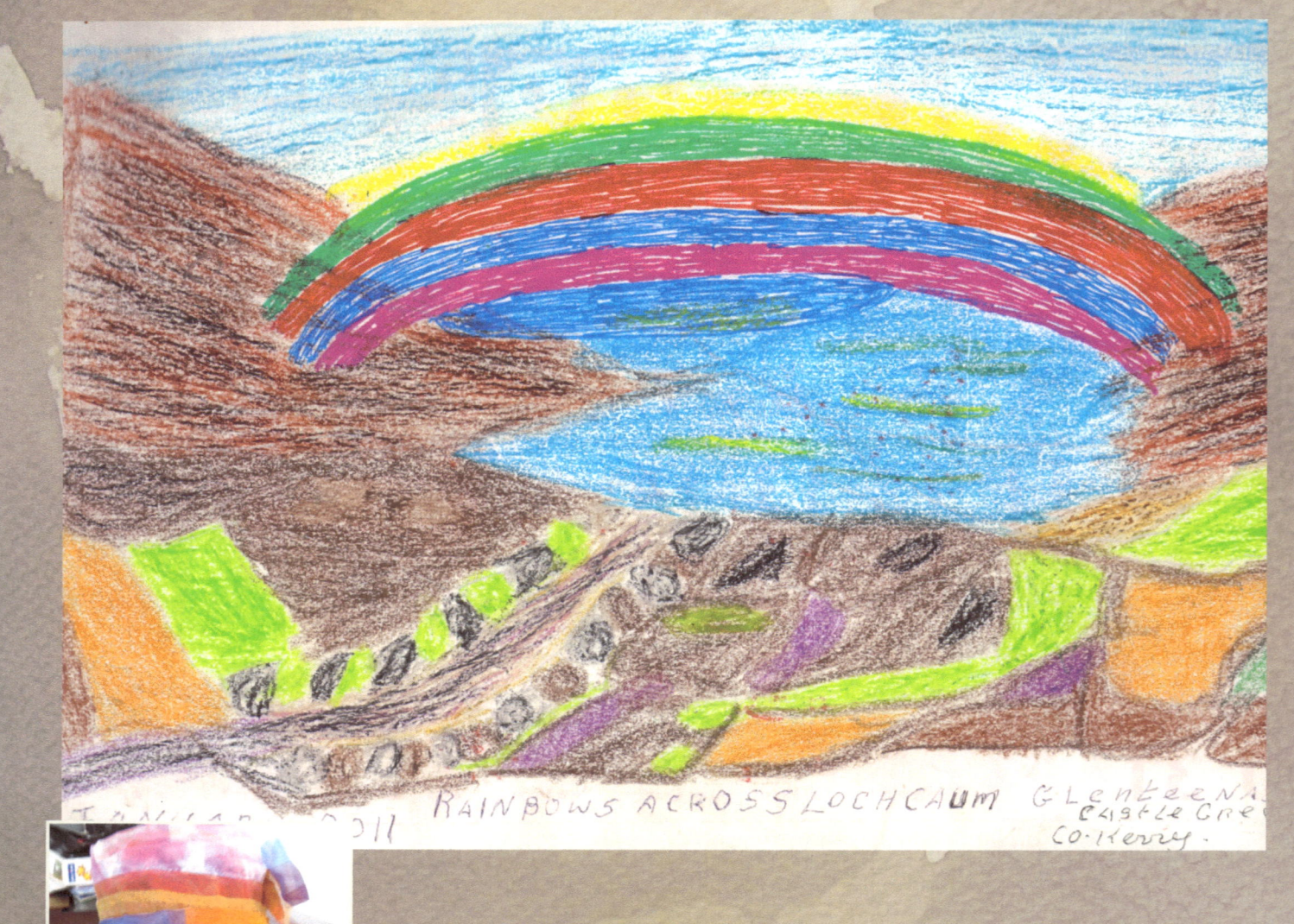

RAINBOWS ACROSS LOCH CAUM GLenteenA
CAstle Cre
Co. Kerry.

Ellen O'Donnell

Ellen was a visiting member of the Wednesday group during the time she spent in Dingle town. Her ability to lovingly evoke vivid scenes, working from memory alone, has left a legacy of highly skilled and vibrant drawings, capturing both the local landscape and everyday scenes from her childhood.

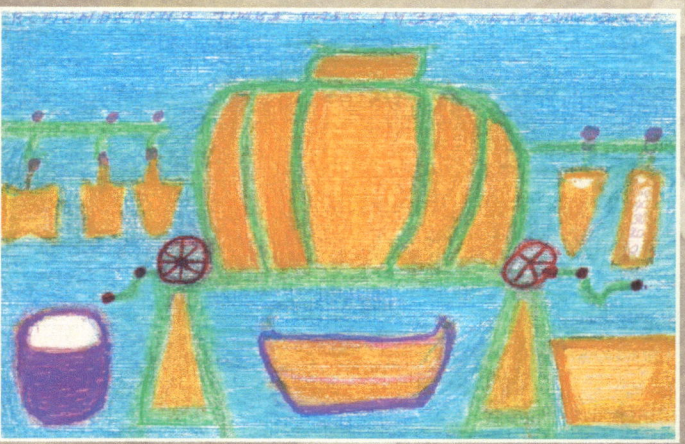

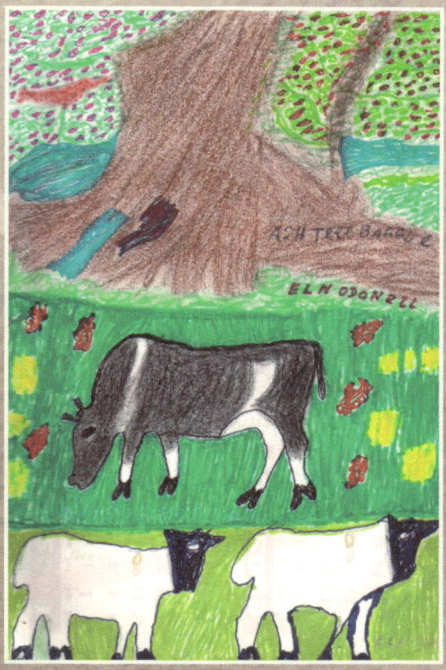

The Butter Barrel

This is away back now in the 30s,
when visitors came out from Tralee,
and my mother had her butter in the barrel.
She had to stop right there;
she was entertaining then.
Course I went out,
and oh, I thought I was grand,
wheeling the barrel.
It was alright at first.
Before I had finished
I swore I'd never again
catch the barrel in my hand.
She came out then,
for all I had it done for her anyway.
In and out of the water
and strained well and everything,
with a couple of leaves of cabbage
to put around it
to take it to the market.

Ellen O'Donnell

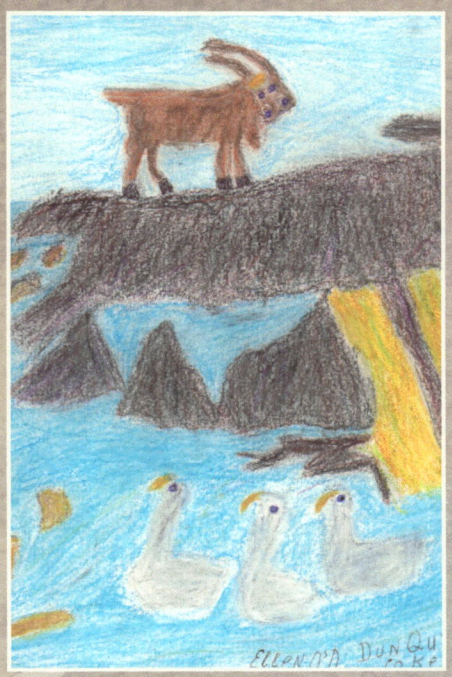

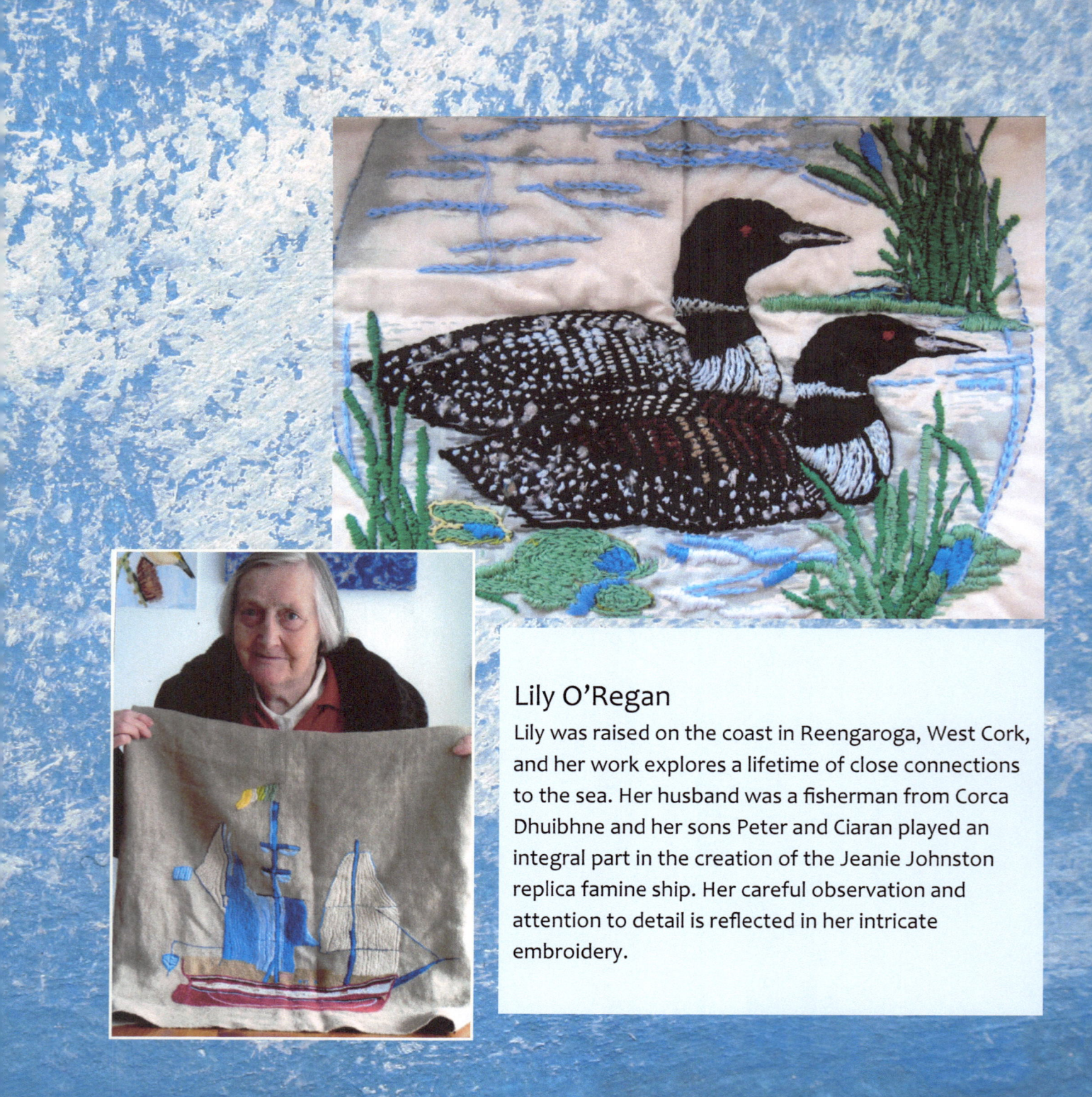

Lily O'Regan

Lily was raised on the coast in Reengaroga, West Cork, and her work explores a lifetime of close connections to the sea. Her husband was a fisherman from Corca Dhuibhne and her sons Peter and Ciaran played an integral part in the creation of the Jeanie Johnston replica famine ship. Her careful observation and attention to detail is reflected in her intricate embroidery.

As a thirteen year old, Lily recorded some of the folklore and traditional crafts of her local area, as part of the Schools' Folklore Scheme.

Lil Ní Leanáin (13 bl.) a fuair na scéalta seo leanas ón a athair Peadar ó Leanáin, Dún na nGall Thiar, Rinngeróige.

Timpeall 80 blian ó shin do chónaig fear in Oidhneán Rinngaróige darbh ainm Tom Long. Bhí stór mór aige agus do cheannaíodh sé cruithneacht agus prataí ós na daoine agus do chuireadh sé isteach san stór iad. Níor thug sé puinn airgid dos na daoine riamh. Do thagadh longa móra agus do thógaidís an cruithneacht agus na prataí thar farraige. In aice an stóir sin tá na "Burned Houses" mar a ghlaodar orthu. Bhí fir ina gconaí ann fadó a bhíodh ag obair ar an bhfeirm. B'é O Dalaigh an duine deireannach a bhí ann. Lá amháin do chuaigh sé go dtí Scibrín, nuair a tháinig sé abhaile bhí a thigh dóite. Do thóg muintear an oileáin tigh eile dó i bpáirc le Micheál O Ceadagáin.

Long ago there lived a woman in a hut in Reengaroga near the spot where my house is now situated. She lived alone and before she died she buried the pot of gold which she always kept and it is said the sun will shine with some beautiful colour one day on the spot where she buried it.

"In my house there is an old spinning wheel which was in use about forty years ago. My father and mother remember quite well to see the flax growing here in Reengaroga."

Lil Ní Leanáin (1937)

About five miles from Skibbereen is a lake called Lough Ine. An old story is told about an old woman who lived there. It is said that she used be always praying alone. Boats used to pass Tráigh na mBó and the sailors used shout at this holy woman and disturb her. A big disaster happened. A great storm arose and they were all drowned. Then a big cliff fell in and this opening is the channel going into Lough Ine.

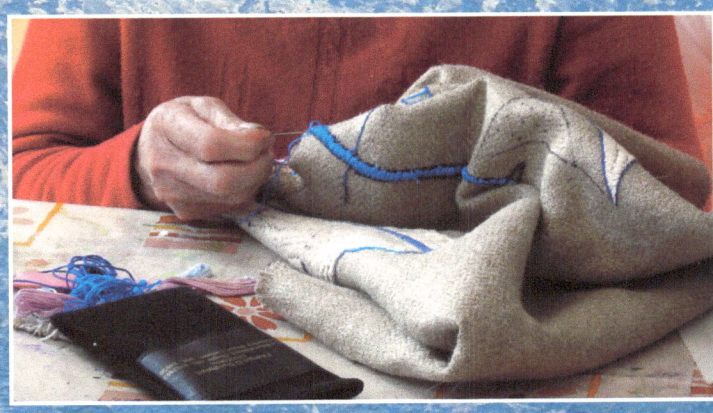

Nóra NicGearailt

Nóra was brought up in a tradition of hard work, and this is reflected in the attention she gave to every piece of art and in the empathetic way she loved to share authentic skills from the past with others. Her love of horses and of rural life lives on in her work.

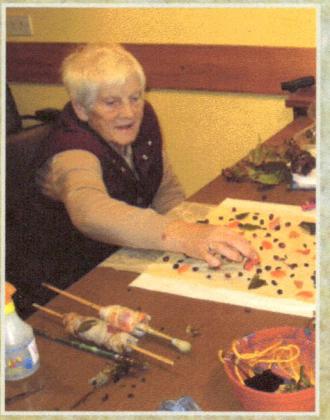

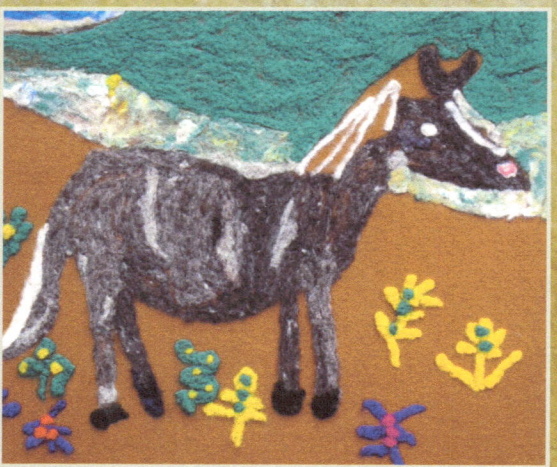

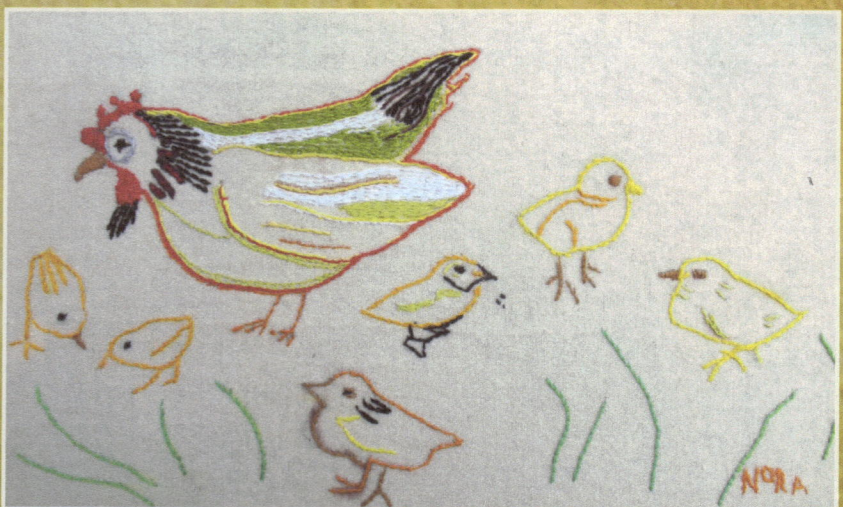

Nora Nic Gearailt ag caint faoin béile ubh a bhíodh acu ar maidin Domhnach Cásca.

Na h-uibh a ithfimís?
Oighean mór graoi. Oighean.
Chuirtí an t-oighean ar an dtine agus líntí í do uibheacha.
Bhíodh ana chuid uibh inti.
An mó ceann a íosfaidh tusa?
An mo ceann a íosfaidh tusa?
An mó ceann a íosfaidh tusa?
Iosfad 5 cinn
Iosfad 6 cinn
O a Mhuire Mháthair, arsa mise, ní bheadh an méid sin ceart!
D'ithfidís an méid sin. D'ithfidís an méid sin. Na buachaillí.
6 cinn.
7 cinn.
Ní gheobhfá an t-ubh ach anois is arís.
D'ithfimís na h-uibh mar ní raibh aon Carghas ar do thigh.
Easter Sunday bheadh cead agat an méid sin d'ithe,agus ní dheinidís breoite aon duine agus chaithfidís dul go dtí an Aifreann taréis seo.
Agus bhíodh mo mháthair scanraithe, beannacht Dé lena anam, scannraithe go mbéidís ag cuir amach.
Ní rabhadar ná iad. Ní rabhadar.
Ach bhíomar go sásta. . . mar ní gheobhfá na huibh i gconaí in aon chor.

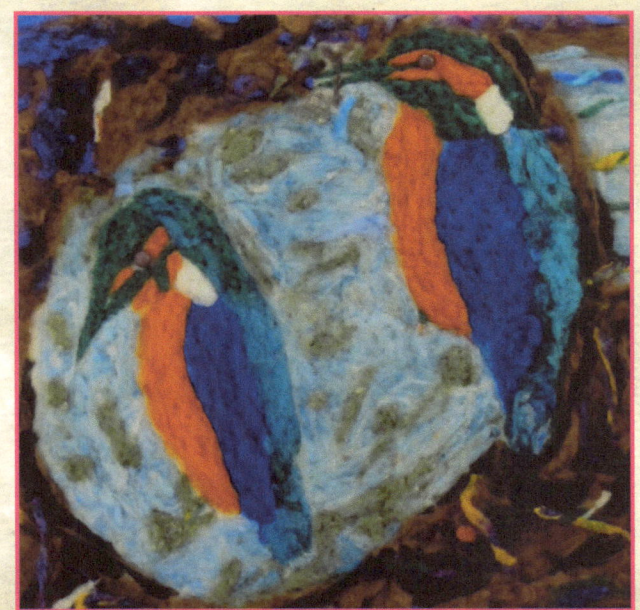

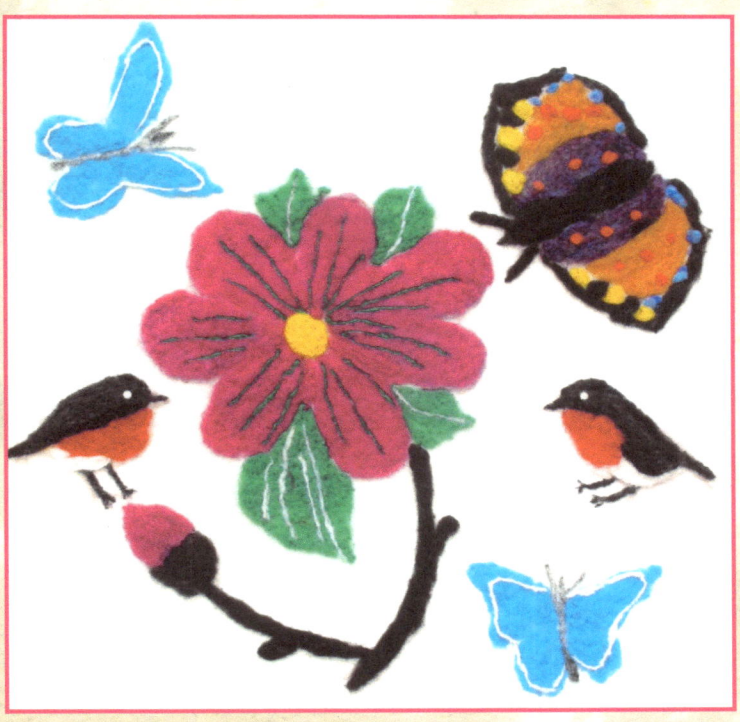

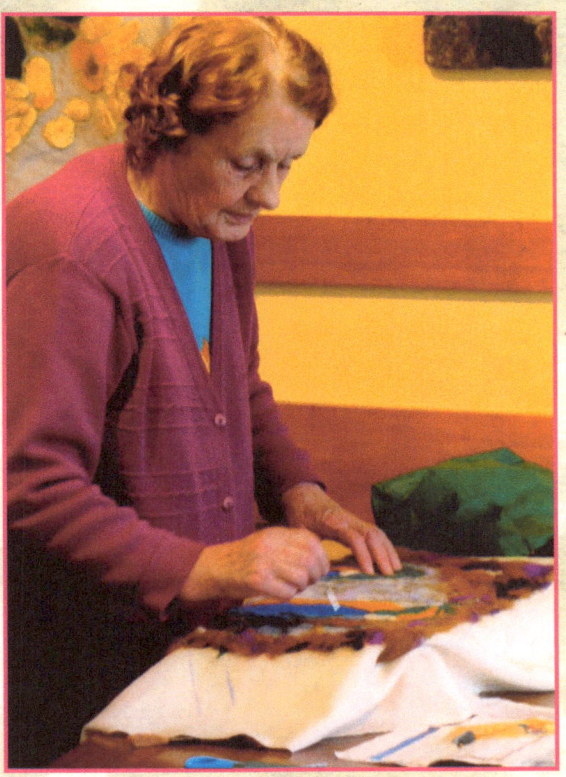

Maryanne Landers

Maryanne's work springs from her intense engagement with the natural environment. She observes all wildlife, but particularly birds, acutely and is intensely aware of them. She has a very particular way of working that demonstrates her nature as a true artist, eclectically gathering materials from everyday life for her work, gathering inspiration from several different sources and combining them to design each piece.

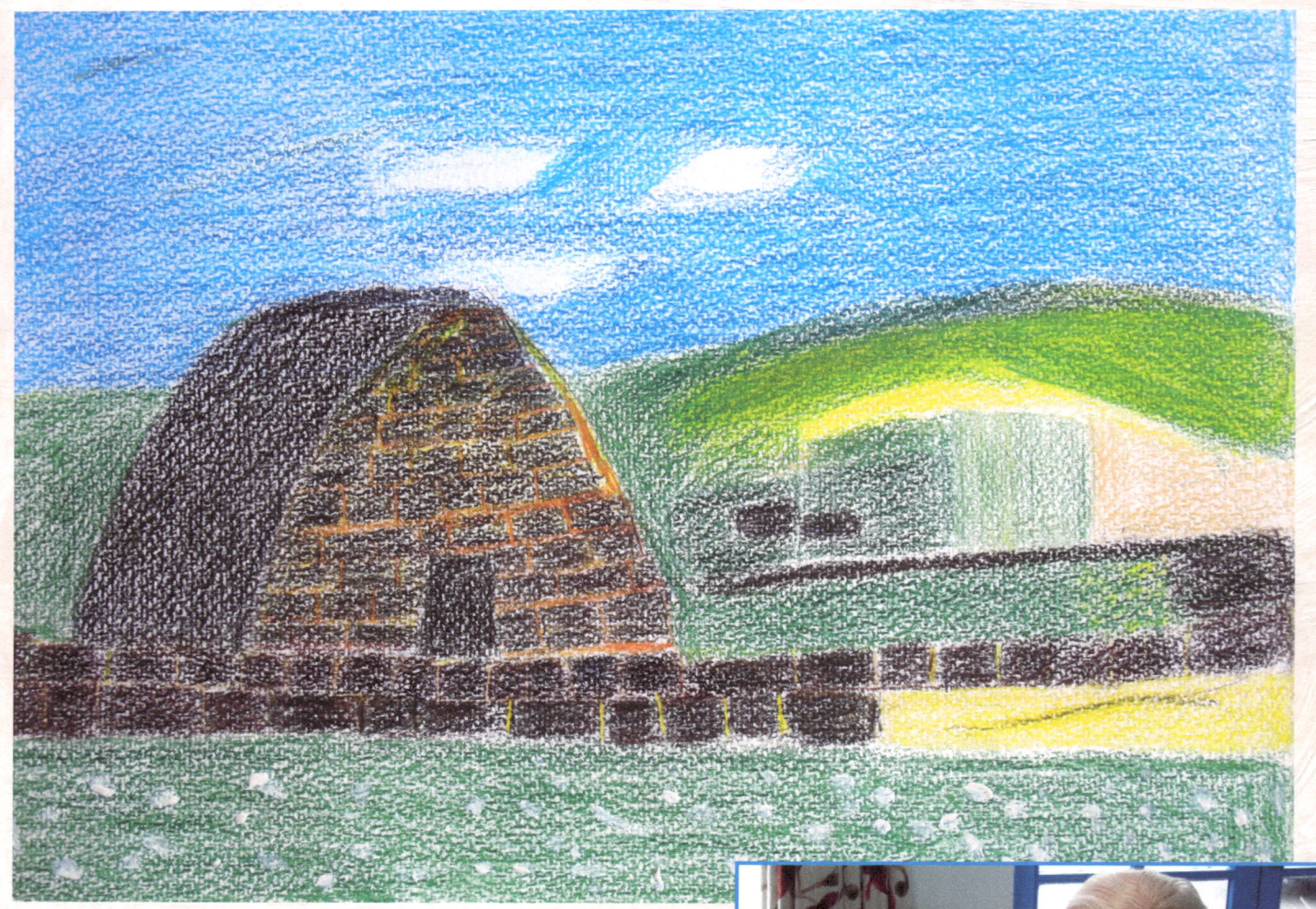

Mícheál O Séaghdha

Having spent many years in Chicago before returning to Corca Dhuibhne, Mícheál bases much of his work on images from the local area that hold authentic meaning for him.

He painstakingly blends individual shapes, tones and shadows to create works of intricacy and beauty.

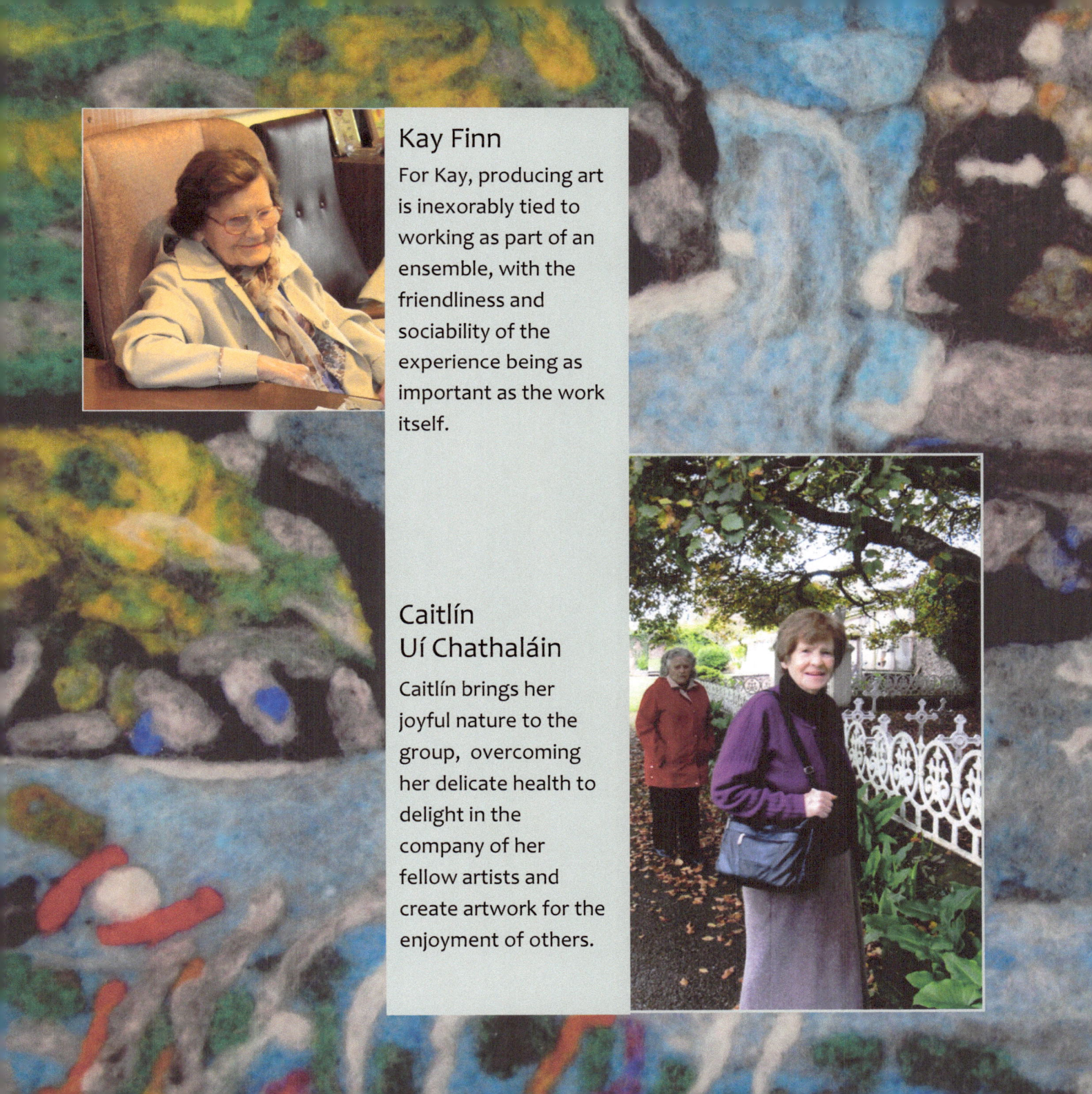

Kay Finn

For Kay, producing art is inexorably tied to working as part of an ensemble, with the friendliness and sociability of the experience being as important as the work itself.

Caitlín Uí Chathaláin

Caitlín brings her joyful nature to the group, overcoming her delicate health to delight in the company of her fellow artists and create artwork for the enjoyment of others.

Being part of the Wednesday Group has provided opportunities for its members to have their art exhibited within the local community. This an important dimension to their work, allowing them to reach a wider audience and put their skill and artistry on display.

The respect they have for each other as artists is evident in their mutual support during showings of their work, and the delight they share in each other's success and public recognition.

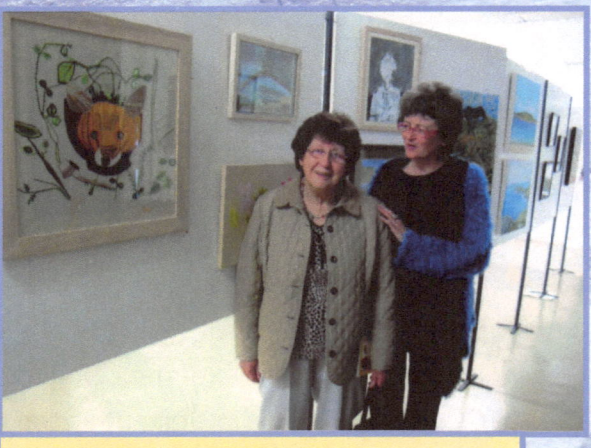

Bealtaine sa Gháirdín

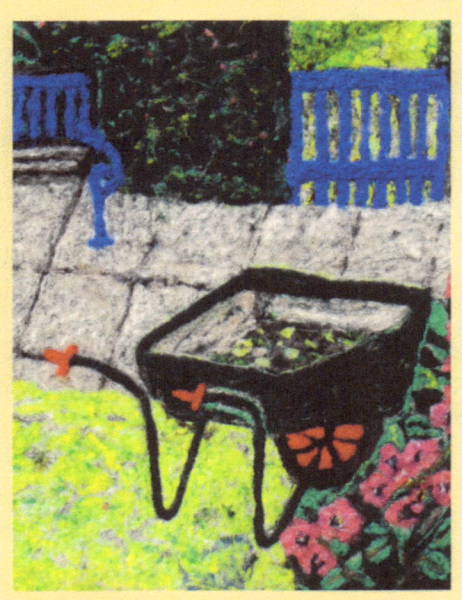

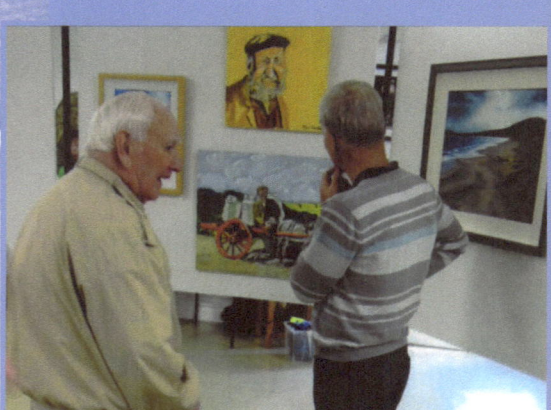

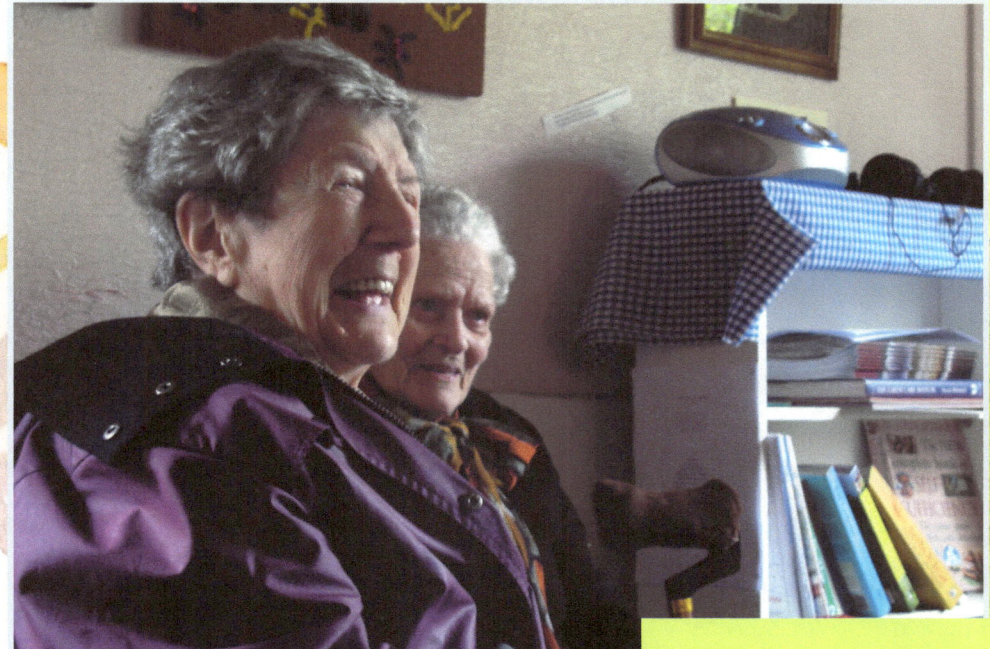

During Féile na Bealtaine Arts Festival in 2012, some of the artists of the Wednesday Group and their friends gathered at the pop-up gallery where their work was being exhibited, to tell stories, share their knowledge of local culture and to relate their own experiences.

The recording they made that day became part of their exhibition.

"On the first of November,
my mother would always have the holy water
I suppose they used to say
the fairies were around or something.
She used to close the door;
bless the door.
She'd take a loaf of bread,
and a mouthful out of it, and say,
'Donas amach agus sonas isteach
Beannacht Dé le anamacha na marbh.'
Happiness in,
bad things out,
bless this house
and have mercy on the dead."

Bríd Ní Shéaghdha

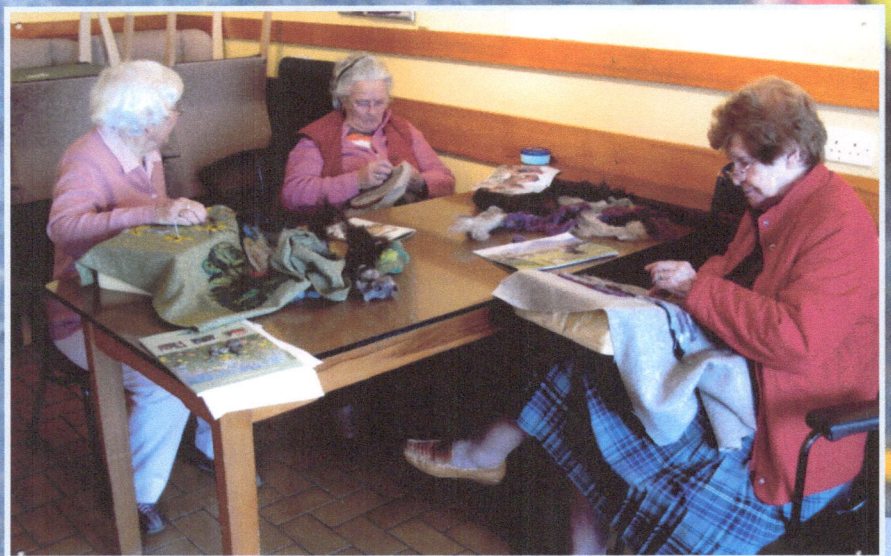

The art of the Wednesday Group is not only characterised by its combination of artistry and utility, but also by the fact that a significant body of work, created over several years, has been widely dispersed throughout the local community and farther afield—to adult children, to friends who visit the area and to international fans who come across their work.

They have designed and created many pieces for display in public buildings, including the local community hospital.

Each work of the Wednesday Group is a gift in the making, ready to be relinquished as soon as it is done, freeing the artists to concentrate on their next project.

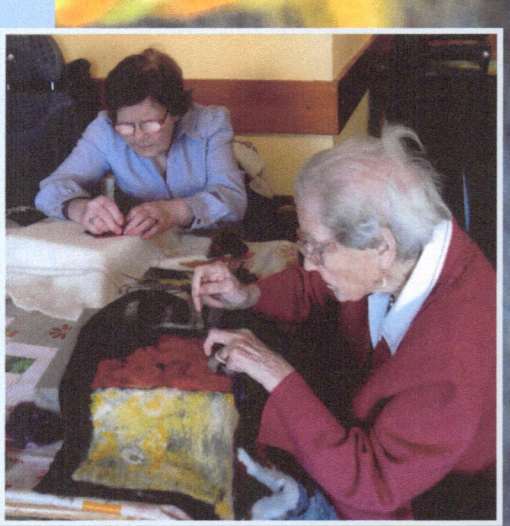

Buíochas

Táimíd buíoch do ghach éinne a chabhraigh linn an imleabhar seo, cuid don sraith 'Bealaí Ealaíona' a chuir le chéile go speisialta:

An foireann in Ionad Lae Ghairdín Mhuire;

Ealaín na Gaeltachta a thugann tacaíocht do tograí ealaíona i nGairdín Mhuire;

Oifig Ealaíona Chomhairle Contae Chiarraí;

Bord Oideachais agus Oiliúna Chiarraí;

agus na ealaíontóirí ar fad.

Go raibh míle maith agaibh!

www.ingramcontent.com/pod-product-compliance
Lightning Source LLC
Chambersburg PA
CBHW040757200526
45159CB00026B/2898